SINGULARITY DUAL-ASPECT EMERGENCE

Volume IV

The Practice Book: Living in Resonance with the Spirit Field

Aston Farquharson

NuSpecies Press

Pawling, New York

2026

The Practice Book: Living in Resonance with the Spirit Field

Copyright © 2026 Aston Farquharson

Published by NuSpecies Press

Pawling, New York, USA

nuspecies.com | aston@nuspecies.com

Volume IV companion edition

eBook ISBN: 979-8-9959594-9-6

Paperback ISBN: 979-8-9960439-0-3

Hardcover ISBN: 979-8-9960439-1-0

First Edition

This book presents the practical and contemplative dimension of Singularity Dual-Aspect Emergence (SDAE). It is a guide to reflection, coherence, daily practice, and resilience. It is not a substitute for medical, psychiatric, legal, or emergency care. Scientific language in this volume is educational and metaphorical where stated; it should not be read as a claim of new physics or guaranteed therapeutic outcomes.

Preface to Volume IV

This volume gathers the lived, reflective, and practical side of the SDAE series. Where Volume I introduces the broader cosmological vision, Volume II clarifies the formal metaphysical framework, and Volume III carries the sacred and scriptural voice, Volume IV is the companion for repetition, use, recovery, and daily coherence.

The materials collected here come from the practical layers of the SDAE corpus: Living in Resonance, the Spirit Field lifestyle, the Ten Principles of Cosmic-Spirit Living, the 30-Day Life Coherence Program, daily rituals of alignment, the workbook exercises, affirmations, meditations, and the newer stress-and-resilience teachings gathered under Coherence Under Pressure.

This book does not ask the reader to suspend reason or confuse metaphor with mechanism. It asks for something harder and more humane: steady attention, bodily regulation, truthful self-observation, ecological humility, and compassionate action. It treats coherence not as perfection but as a practice that must be restored again and again.

Some of the material here is explicitly contemplative. Some is educational. Some is practical. None of it should be treated as coercive, heroic, or punitive. Use what helps. Adapt what needs adapting. If a practice destabilizes you, stop and return to gentler ground.

Table of Contents

SDAE begins with a simple truth many NuSpecians already know in their bodies: human health happens at the intersection of Inner Reality and Outer Reality.

- Outer Reality includes environment, workload, medical systems, money stress, discrimination, grief, noise, time pressure, and the daily vigilance that comes from being othered.
- Inner Reality includes emotion, meaning, conscience, attention, spirit, identity, memory, and the capacity to recover after impact.

When those two realities fall out of relationship for too long, people do not only feel stressed; they become stressed in the body. Chronic stress is a whole-body program involving brain signaling, hormones, immune tone, metabolism, cardiovascular strain, and sleep disruption.

Modern physiology names the cumulative burden of repeated stress adaptation allostatic load. SDAE adds a spiritual discipline to that science: you do not only manage stress - you defend coherence. If anyone or anything repeatedly warps the curvature of your spacetime, it does not belong in your orbit.

This section is educational rather than clinical. Its purpose is to help NuSpecians understand why stress feels spiritual, emotional, and biological at the same time - and why small, repeated acts of regulation matter.

Part I — Living in Resonance

The practical and existential side of SDAE: how a dual-aspect being lives in coherence with body, mind, nature, and the larger universe.

1. A Way of Being, Not a Belief

The Spirit Field lifestyle begins from a simple conviction: a person can live in deeper coherence without surrendering science, without attaching themselves to dogma, and without pretending that metaphor is measurement. In this book, Spirit refers to the interior dimension of life when awareness, meaning, compassion, and coherence become organized enough to be felt and practiced.

In this practical sense, "resonance" means alignment: between body and rhythm, between values and action, between relationship and responsibility, between inner stillness and outer participation. A coherent life is not a life without pain; it is a life in which pain does not dictate the entire architecture of the self.

2. The Seven Pillars of the Spirit Field Lifestyle

The Spirit Field lifestyle organizes around seven interlocking pillars: nature, stillness, connection, cosmic awareness, embodied wisdom, meaning and purpose, and ethics of resonance. Together they provide a practical structure for living as a dual-aspect being—one whose body belongs to the physical universe and whose interior life belongs to the universe of meaning.

Returning to Nature

Nature is the first pillar because the body is not separate from the ecological order that formed it. Time outdoors, circadian rhythm, whole-food nourishment, movement, and stewardship all help restore coherence.

Cultivating Inner Stillness

Stillness reduces cognitive noise and emotional turbulence. Slow breathing, silence, mindful attention, and reduced overstimulation help restore sensitivity to interior clarity.

Human Connection

Relationship is a core amplifier of coherence. Empathy, kindness, careful listening, and truthful presence are not optional extras; they are among the clearest expressions of the Spirit Field in daily life.

Cosmic Awareness

Perspective matters. Awe, humility, curiosity, and a scientifically informed sense of belonging to a vast cosmos help loosen narcissism and widen concern.

Embodied Wisdom

The body is the vessel of resonance. Sleep, movement, nourishment, breath, and moderation shape the conditions under which interior life can remain clear.

Meaning and Purpose

Purpose emerges where values, creativity, service, and truthfulness converge. Meaning is not belief alone; it is lived alignment.

Ethics of Resonance

Truthfulness, restraint, compassion, ecological responsibility, and non-cruelty are not imposed commandments here. They are the human consequences of coherence.

3. The Ten Principles of Cosmic-Spirit Living

The ten principles distill the lifestyle into portable guidance. They are designed to be memorable, repeatable, and usable in daily life rather than merely admired as abstract ideals.

1. Live in alignment with nature's rhythm.

2. Cultivate inner stillness to hear the Spirit Field.

3. Treat other beings with compassion and curiosity.

4. Seek scientific understanding as a form of reverence.

5. Live in ecological reciprocity.

6. Practice truthfulness and integrity.

7. Evolve consciously, not just automatically.

8. Seek harmony over domination.

9. Honor mystery without inventing certainty.

10. Love as a cosmic act.

Taken together, these principles describe cosmic-spirit living as a practice of balance: respect for the body, reverence for nature, seriousness about science, humane connection, and openness to the unknown.

4. Cosmic Balance and Inner Balance

Across time, human beings have looked upward and sensed that the sky is not only beautiful but instructive. SDAE does not claim that stars control our emotions or that galaxies directly shape human psychology. Instead, it treats the cosmos as a mirror of pattern: systems gain balance, lose balance, and recover balance again.

Modern cosmology shows that the universe is dynamic. Stars are born, stabilize, and collapse. Galaxies merge and reorganize. Systems gain order and drift toward disorder unless renewed. This becomes a philosophical key for understanding ourselves.

A star remains luminous only through equilibrium: gravity pulling inward, radiant pressure pushing outward. When those forces drift too far apart, the star changes state. Human life is not physically identical to a star, but the pattern is resonant. Balance produces clarity. Imbalance produces transformation. Transformation is not always failure; often it is part of the rhythm of renewal.

Entropy gives the metaphor additional depth. Systems tend toward disorder unless fresh energy enters. In inner life, coherence is not a permanent possession. It must be renewed through rest, reflection, relationship, nourishment, truthful attention, and purpose. This is why SDAE describes inner balance as an ecology rather than a static achievement.

One of the clearest practical teachings emerging from this pattern is what SDAE calls coherent equilibrium: a workable harmony between internal forces and external conditions, not perfect, not static, but sufficient for clarity, dignity, and meaningful living. Coherent equilibrium is flexible, adaptive, cyclical, and deeply human.

5. The Evolutionary Horizon and Conscious Practice

The practice materials place daily coherence inside a larger human story. Humanity can be understood as a threshold phenomenon: biological, cultural, and interior. The outward arc of evolution gives bodies, tools, networks, and civilization. The inward arc gives empathy, moral imagination, symbolic meaning, and coherence. Practice matters because it is one of the places where the inward arc becomes intentional.

For Volume IV, the evolutionary horizon functions as motivation, not metaphysical proof. It reminds the reader that the work of coherence is not only private. How one breathes, rests, listens, and acts also shapes families, communities, and future generations.

Part II — Daily and Relational Practice

Small, repeatable disciplines for body, attention, and relationship.

6. Daily Alignment: Nature, Stillness, and Breath

A daily practice of SDAE coherence begins with small stabilizers rather than heroic gestures. Go outside. Notice the weather. Breathe more slowly than your stress would prefer. Return to light in the morning, steadier food rhythms, and brief intervals of silence. The aim is not perfection but calibration: repeatedly bringing the body and attention back into intelligible relation with themselves.

7. Relational Coherence and Community

The Spirit Field is strengthened through relationship. Empathy, careful listening, non-cruelty, truthful presence, and quiet reciprocity all become forms of practical coherence. Relational damage is never merely social; it becomes part of the inner climate. Communities of coherence need not be large. They can begin with one safe person, one repeated act of kindness, one reduction of unnecessary harm, one honest conversation.

8. Truthfulness, Integrity, Purpose, and Ethical Resonance

Truth is alignment with reality; integrity is alignment between action, intention, and values. In practice, purpose is discovered where values, creativity, service, and honest self-knowledge converge. Ethical resonance therefore includes restraint, compassion, ecological reciprocity, and responsibility. These are not performances; they are conditions that strengthen coherence.

Part III — The 30-Day SDAE Life Coherence Program

A daily journey into harmony between the outer universe and the inner Spirit Field. Flexible, gentle, and non-dogmatic.

9. Week One — Awakening to Dual-Aspect Identity

Theme: "I am the meeting place of matter and experience." Focus: basic awareness, emotional grounding, and reconnection with nature and the cosmos.

Day 1 — The Two Universes Meditation

Look at the sky or an image of it for five minutes.

Say: "There is an outer universe and an inner universe. I belong to both."

Day 2 — Embodied Stardust Practice

Touch your heartbeat.

Reflect: Every atom in me was forged in a star.

Journal: "How does this change how I see myself?"

Day 3 — Spirit Field Awareness

Observe three emotions without judging them.

Label each: "A feeling is arising within my field."

Day 4 — Nature Reconnection Walk

Take a 15-minute walk outdoors.

Notice one natural pattern and ask: "What does this reveal about the universe's outward unfolding?"

Day 5 — Breath of Expansion

Breathe in for four seconds, pause for two, exhale for six.

Imagine the breath as a metaphor for expansion and release.

Day 6 — The Quiet Witness

Sit for five minutes.

Watch thoughts as passing visitors.

Say: "I am the space they pass through."

Day 7 — Weekly Integration Reflection

Write one page answering: What did I notice about my outer world? What did I notice about my inner world? Where did the two aspects touch?

10. Week Two — Cultivating Outer-Inner Balance

Theme: "Life flourishes when structure and coherence grow together." Focus: body care, emotional alignment, and environmental awareness.

Day 8 — Physical Structure Ritual

Do gentle stretching, yoga, or another modest movement practice.

Say: "This is the universe maintaining its structure through me."

Day 9 — Nourishment Gratitude Pause

Before eating, pause and recognize a chain of support: soil, plant, sun, water, hands, plate.

Day 10 — Inner Coherence Scan

Scan your body from toes to head.

Label tension as outer imbalance and confusion as inner imbalance. Breathe into both.

Day 11 — Elemental Contact Ritual

Touch water, stone, earth, or wind.

Ask: "How old is this? What universe shaped it?"

Day 12 — Emotional Integration Practice

Choose one strong emotion from the day.

Ask: What is its message? Is it protecting me? What does it need?

Day 13 — The Reciprocal Gesture

Perform one act that benefits nature or another person: plant something, reduce waste, help someone anonymously.

Day 14 — Weekly Integration Reflection

Write: When did I feel most aligned? What physical practices supported my mind? What inner practices supported my body?

11. Week Three — Expanding Consciousness and Compassion

Theme: "The Spirit Field deepens when I learn to see others as expressions of the same origin." Focus: empathy, ethics, connectedness, and existential meaning.

Day 15 — Relational Spirit Field Practice

In one conversation today, listen without preparing replies. Feel the shared human interiority.

Day 16 — Cosmological Humility Ritual

Look at a night sky or an image.

Whisper: "My concerns matter, but they are not the whole universe."

Recall someone who is suffering.

Wish silently: "May you find peace."

Write one meaningful moment from your life.

Ask: "How did both my physical world and inner world shape this?"

Choose one ethical principle—patience, honesty, or kindness—and practice it consciously for 24 hours.

Imagine awareness expanding outward: room, building, city, planet, cosmos. Then inward: body, breath, heart, thoughts, presence.

Answer: How has my empathy expanded? What new insights emerged? Where did inner and outer worlds meet this week?

12. Week Four — Living as a Coherent Cosmic Being
Theme: "To live well is to align with both arcs of the universe." Focus: purpose, sustained habits, longevity of mind and body, and integrated life.

Write three values and three goals.

Ask: "How does each serve both outer structure and inner coherence?"

Choose one longevity-positive action: a 30-minute walk, better sleep, less sugar, or hydration focus.

Say: "My body is my link to the physical universe."

Choose one mind-coherence action: a mindful break, journaling, reading philosophy, or a deep conversation.

Say: "My mind is my expression of the inner universe."

Write a one-page dialogue where "the universe" asks: What are you learning? What do you fear? What are you becoming?

For one day, behave as if your actions ripple outward across human and planetary systems.

Take 20 to 30 minutes alone.

Ask: What am I shedding? What am I growing into?

If your life taught one lesson to future humans, what would it be? Write it as one sentence.

Rate outer harmony from 1 to 10 and inner harmony from 1 to 10. Write two actions to raise each score.

Light a candle or imagine one.

Say: "I am a child of the outer universe of structure. I am a child of the inner universe of spirit. In me, the two become one. May I live with coherence, compassion, and clarity."

Sit in silence for one minute and close the program with a sense of arrival and beginning.

Part IV — Rituals of Coherence

13. Morning Alignment and Nature Immersion

Morning Alignment Ritual: Face an open sky or a window. Recognize the vast outward universe. Place a hand on your chest and recognize the inward universe. Whisper: "I am the meeting place of the inner and outer cosmos." This establishes dual-aspect awareness at the start of the day.

Nature Immersion Ritual: Spend 10 to 15 minutes outdoors. Observe one natural pattern—water, branches, clouds, insects, stones, or soil. Ask: "How is this structure an expression of the universe's outward unfolding?" Place yourself in the continuity: "This, too, is my origin."

14. Spirit Field Coherence and Internal Witnessing

Spirit Field Coherence Ritual: Sit comfortably and recall three emotional states from the day—one joyful, one stressful, one neutral. Bring them together without judging them. Imagine them settling into one integrated inner field. This practice strengthens emotional integration and interior coherence.

The Ritual of Internal Witnessing: Observe a thought as if it were happening in a distant room. Say: "A thought is arising in consciousness." Do the same with emotions: "An emotion is visiting my field." Notice the difference between you and the mental event. This practice strengthens the witness rather than the reaction.

15. Rhythmic Breathing, Nourishment, and Night Sky Practice

Rhythmic Breathing Ritual: Inhale for four seconds, hold for two, exhale for six. Repeat five to ten times. In SDAE language, this mirrors cosmic expansion only metaphorically. Its practical purpose is simpler: slower breathing can support calm, perspective, and resilience.

Mindful Nourishment Ritual: Before eating, pause with your food. Acknowledge its lineage—sunlight, photosynthesis, soil minerals, water, biological life cycles. Whisper: "This is the universe sustaining my form." The aim is gratitude and healthier attention, not dietary dogma.

Night Sky Ritual: Spend a minute or more looking at the night sky or an image of it. Reflect that stars forged the atoms in your body, dark matter helps hold galaxies together, and consciousness allows the cosmos to be known. Think: "The universe expresses itself outward and inward. I belong to both."

16. Reciprocity, Evening Integration, and Weekly Renewal

Reciprocity Ritual: Choose one act that gives back—to nature, to community, or to another person. Pick up litter, help someone without credit, donate, volunteer, or plant something. Say: "As the universe supports me, I support the universe."

Evening Integration Ritual: Ask two questions: What structure did I build today? What coherence did I cultivate today? End by saying: "Both arcs unfolded through me today."

Weekly Renewal Ritual: Once a week, spend 15 to 20 minutes in three movements: a body scan, a gratitude list, and a reading or reflection from cosmology, nature writing, or philosophy. The purpose is to reconnect the physical and experiential aspects through repetition.

17. The SDAE Premise: Inner Reality and Outer Reality

SDAE begins with a simple truth many NuSpecians already know in their bodies: human health happens at the intersection of Inner Reality and Outer Reality. Outer Reality includes environment, workload, money stress, medical systems, grief, discrimination, noise, and the daily pressures of navigating an unequal world. Inner Reality includes emotion, meaning, conscience, attention, spirit, memory, identity, and the ability to recover after impact.

When those two realities fall out of relationship for too long, people do not only feel stressed; they become stressed in the body. One of the most useful practical teachings in this section is simple: if anyone or anything repeatedly warps the curvature of your life, it may not belong in your orbit. Modern physiology has language for the cumulative burden of repeated stress adaptation. SDAE adds a discipline of dignity to that science: you do not only manage stress—you defend coherence.

18. Black NuSpecians' Coherence Blessing

This chapter is written in honor of what many Black NuSpecians have reported over decades of conversation: stress from racism and discrimination, stress from not being heard or believed, stress from doing everything right while still being metabolically and emotionally taxed, and stress that often remains private even inside families.

SDAE treats these testimonies not as weakness, but as human data with moral weight. The science of allostatic load and weathering helps describe how repeated exposure, vigilance, humiliation, and threat without control can become biologically expensive over time.

Health disparity is real, and it is not a character flaw. Differences in health outcomes across groups are shaped by access, environment, care quality, economic strain, diagnostic delay, cumulative vigilance, and the burden of being othered. The lesson is not blame. The lesson is that Outer Reality can become physiologically costly, and no one should have to be heroic simply to remain well.

Naming matters. Some stress is not poor coping; it is exposure. Naming is coherence. Silence is not always peace; sometimes it is compression. A coherence blessing for this reality begins with truth: what is wounding you should be named honestly, not spiritualized away.

- Reduce the vigilance tax where you can: lower needless exposure to humiliation cycles, rage-trigger media, and destabilizing environments.
- Build safe rooms and safe people: relationships, clinicians, communities, and practices that do not demand self-erasure.
- Create post-impact rituals: breath, shower, music, prayer, walking, journaling, silence, or one call to someone who steadies you.

SDAE translation: Outer pressure becomes inner curvature. If it bends your time, it bends your physiology. But dignity can still be protected. Stability is not denial. Coherence is not weakness. Resonance is not fantasy. It is how the human spirit keeps its shape.

19. The SDAE Stress Protocol

The practical stress protocol in Volume IV is deliberately small. It is designed to help a person regain stability without pretending that life is easy.

S — Stabilize the body

Choose one or two actions that bring the nervous system out of immediate overload.

- Five physiological sighs or three to five minutes of slow breathing.
- Hydration and morning light, if appropriate for your health situation.
- Ten to twenty minutes of walking, chair-walking, gentle stepping, or another calm movement practice.
- Sleep protection: a consistent bedtime, reduced late scrolling, and a cooler, darker room.

SDAE rule: you cannot think your way out of a dysregulated body.

D — Discern the stressor

Name the pressure honestly.

- The stressor is _____.
- What I can control today is _____.
- What I cannot control today is _____.
- What boundary would reduce warping is _____.

A — Align with values

Stress becomes toxic when the self is forced to betray itself daily. Alignment can be small but real.

- Ask one question you have been afraid to ask your clinician.
- Schedule one supportive conversation or community contact.
- Create one protected hour this week for rest, reflection, or order.
- Make one advocacy move: a second opinion, a written symptom timeline, or a patient-support step.

E — Elevate the spirit

Not performance. Not positivity. Elevation.

- Prayer, if that is your path.
- Three things that held me today.
- Forgiveness as unclenching, not excusing harm.
- A dignity paragraph: I want to be remembered for _____.

The point is repetition. Small acts, repeated, help restore a system that has been over-bent.

20. Protective Boundaries, Orbit Management, and Dignity

Orbit Management is a NuSpecian phrase for reducing avoidable sources of chronic stress. It means protecting inner spacetime before exhaustion becomes collapse.

- Set boundaries with people who repeatedly destabilize you.
- Reduce unnecessary noise, conflict, overstimulation, and media flooding.

- Protect sleep, mealtimes, quiet time, and relationships that support steadiness.
- Choose environments, routines, and communities that lower chronic strain where possible.

NuSpecian stress teaching also begins with Vagus Support and gentle movement. Slow deep breathing, mindfulness, light stretching, and walking are not minor practices; they are ways of lowering overload so the inner field is easier to steady. Movement helps the body re-enter rhythm. Rest, nutrition, sleep, and supportive relationships belong to stress regulation first, not last.

The deeper principle here is dignity. If cure is not available, care still is. If pressure is unavoidable, coherence can still be protected. Boundaries, support, truth-telling, and self-protection are part of spiritual practice, not selfishness.

If it warps your spacetime, it does not belong in your orbit.

Part VI — Stress Chemistry and Stress Physics
A science-grounded explanation of how chronic stress changes the body over time.

21. The Two Master Stress Systems
Most stress biology runs through two coupled systems.

The fast system: sympathetic nervous system
The sympathetic nervous system releases catecholamine-driven signals that rapidly shift heart rate, vigilance, blood pressure, and fuel availability. It is the body's immediate mobilization program.

The slower system: hypothalamic–pituitary–adrenal axis
The HPA axis drives cortisol secretion. Cortisol changes gene expression and metabolism over minutes to hours and normally follows a circadian rhythm. Under chronic stress, that rhythm can become dysregulated.

In healthy cycles, these systems rise when needed and then resolve. Under chronic pressure, especially when the pressure includes persistent vigilance, humiliation, or threat without control, they may remain over-engaged. That is part of what stress researchers describe as cumulative physiological wear and tear.

22. Energy Re-Budgeting, Metabolism, and Inflammation
A useful physics lens treats stress as energy re-budgeting. Under threat, the body reprioritizes immediate ATP availability, rapid glucose release, lipid mobilization, cardiovascular delivery, and short-term survival.

Catecholamines act quickly through receptor signaling and second-messenger pathways. One major consequence is lipolysis: the release of fatty acids and glycerol from adipose tissue. Cortisol acts more slowly through gene regulation, increasing hepatic glucose production and shifting lipid and protein metabolism in ways that may be adaptive during emergency but harmful when persistent.

The metabolic signature of chronic stress can include higher glucose output, impaired insulin signaling, altered lipid handling, ectopic fat deposition, and protein breakdown used as emergency substrate. In practical terms, this helps explain why chronic stress overlaps so often with metabolic drift, sleep disruption, digestion problems, and inflammatory bias.

Inflammation belongs in this chapter because cortisol is not only a stress hormone; it is also part of the body's braking system. When chronic stress deforms the system for long enough, that brake can become less effective. The result may be a persistent inflammatory tilt. This does not mean every disease is caused by stress. It means stress can amplify biological vulnerability.

SDAE translation: stress is not merely emotion. It is a systems-level reallocation of fuel, signaling, and repair capacity.

23. Mitochondria, Aging, and the Long Arc of Stress

If you want one concept that unites chemistry and physics in the stress story, it is mitochondria. Mitochondria convert nutrients into ATP, regulate reactive oxygen species, shape inflammatory signaling, and participate in cell-survival and recovery programs.

This helps connect chronic stress to fatigue, metabolic dysregulation, inflammatory amplification, and the long arc of biological wear. When energy production and energy allocation remain chronically distorted, coherence often collapses at the cellular level before symptoms become fully legible.

Stress also changes the body's relationship with time. Telomere research is not destiny, but it does suggest that long, repeated stress exposure can affect the body's maintenance signals across time. SDAE translation: chronic stress does not only hurt today; it can bend the long arc of biological resilience.

A careful teaching point belongs here: stress is best understood as a risk amplifier and a resilience reducer, not as a single cause of complex illness. It is reasonable to say chronic stress biology can influence immune tone, metabolism, fatigue, inflammation, and aspects of disease progression in some contexts. It is not responsible to say stress alone explains everything.

24. Knowledge, Agency, and Coherent Action

SDAE treats education as an intervention on Inner Reality that changes Outer Reality choices. Knowledge restores agency. Agency enables repetition. Repetition builds coherence. Coherence improves recovery.

A simple teaching model closes the section:

- Stress -> Signals -> Substrates -> Structure -> Symptoms
- Signals: cortisol, catecholamines, autonomic activation.
- Substrates: glucose, fatty acids, amino acids, inflammatory mediators.
- Structure: mitochondria, immune tone, vascular tone, sleep architecture, digestion.
- Symptoms: fatigue, dysregulation, mood strain, flares, metabolic drift, slower repair.

SDAE adds one final line to that model: what bends your time can bend your biology. That is why knowledge matters. It turns vague fear into concrete action and helps people choose steadier sleep, gentler movement, better boundaries, more coherent nourishment, and stronger support.

Volume IV does not present these ideas as medical replacement. It presents them as a practice of coherence: body, mind, spirit, and environment brought back into workable relationship - again and again.

25. Diagram Practices and Reflective Exercises

Tracing a Moment Across Both Aspects: choose a recent experience and describe it twice—first in outer terms (actions, setting, events, conditions), then in inner terms (emotion, meaning, memory, interpretation, value). Ask where the two aspects touched.

The Coherence Cycle: identify which is easiest for you and which is most blocked—structural stability, emotional clarity, meaning alignment, relational connection, or ethical action. Write one repair step for the weakest area.

One Relationship, Two Universes: choose someone important. Write how this person affects your Spirit Field, how you affect theirs, one helping influence, one stressful influence, and one practical boundary or repair.

The Three Horizons of Human Growth: rank structural health, Spirit Field coherence, and community contribution in order of present importance. Then write one growth step for each horizon.

Trace My Lineage of Meaning: use the continuum Cosmos → Stars → Planets → Life → Brain → Spirit → Meaning → Action → Legacy. Write one sentence for each stage, ending with one small action for today.

26. Weekly Integration and Life Mapping

The Alignment Triangle: for Body, Spirit, and Relationships, write what is shaping each one today. Then identify one small shift toward alignment.

My One-Page Life Map: summarize your present situation through four headings—Structure, Spirit Field, Humanity, Lifestyle. Ask what outer factors shape your reality, what inner truths shape your response, what relationships stabilize you, and what one next step would increase coherence.

The Workbook of Coherence is not a diagnostic instrument. It is a companion for awareness, emotional clarity, relational honesty, and humane self-understanding.

Part VIII — Affirmations and Meditations
Short forms for repetition, steadiness, and reflective use.

27. Affirmations of the Spirit Field

Inner Stillness
I return to the stillness within me, where Spirit awakens.

In every breath, I find clarity.

Peace is my natural state; I relax into it.

My thoughts quiet, and my awareness expands.

I am present, grounded, and whole.

Connection and Compassion
I recognize myself in all beings; empathy flows freely.

Compassion strengthens me; kindness aligns me with the universe.

What I give to the world returns as resonance within me.

Every gentle act amplifies the Spirit Field in my life.

I walk with softness, knowing all things are connected.

Cosmic Awareness
I am made of stars; the cosmos lives in me.

I am a conscious expression of the universe's unfolding.

Wonder opens my mind; humility opens my heart.

The mystery of existence inspires my path.

I belong to the vast and beautiful story of the cosmos.

Purpose and Evolution
I choose growth, clarity, and conscious evolution.

My actions carry meaning; my choices shape my future.

I cultivate wisdom, courage, and honesty in all things.

I evolve with intention—mind, body, and Spirit in harmony.

I am becoming the best version of my cosmic self.

Nature is my teacher; I listen with respect.

I breathe with the Earth; we are one rhythm.

Every step I take honors the planet that carries me.

Living simply connects me to the Spirit Field.

I am part of the living web, balanced and grateful.

I am steady, centered, and anchored in truth.

Challenges awaken deeper wisdom within me.

My inner light remains constant in all circumstances.

I trust my journey, for the Spirit Field walks with me.

I rise with strength born of clarity and compassion.

28. Strength, Healing, and Clarity

Strength: I am rooted in myself; nothing can shake the core of who I am. Strength rises in me with every breath I take. I face challenges with courage, and courage grows in me daily. My resilience is flexible, steady, and unbreakable. I carry the strength of stars within my bones.

Healing: Healing flows through me with ease and wisdom. I release what no longer serves my well-being. My body knows how to recover; I give it permission to heal. My heart softens; my Spirit strengthens. I am gentle with myself, patient with my process, and kind to my wounds.

Clarity: My mind is clear, calm, and open to truth. Clarity comes easily when I listen to the quiet within. I see my path with growing confidence and understanding. Confusion fades as I return to my center. I make decisions aligned with authenticity and wisdom.

Combined triads: I am strong like the stars, healed like the dawn, and clear like the open sky. My Spirit is grounded, my heart is whole, and my mind is bright. I walk with strength, rest in healing, and act with clarity. The universe moves through me—strong, kind, and wise. I am evolving, renewing, and awakening every day.

29. Meditations of the Spirit Field

Meditation 1 — The Breath of Stillness
Inhale: I receive the calm of the universe.

Exhale: I release the weight I no longer need.

Inhale: I draw in clarity.

Exhale: I settle into peace.

Rest in the silence between breaths—here the Spirit Field begins to speak.

Meditation 2 — The Web of Connection

I feel my heartbeat—this is nature within me.

I breathe the air of countless beings—this is unity within me.

I open to compassion—this is Spirit within me.

I walk gently—this is wisdom within me.

I am part of everything, and everything is part of me.

Meditation 3 — The Cosmic Perspective

Above me are the stars that made my bones.

Around me is the universe unfolding its story.

Within me is awareness—the universe becoming conscious.

I am small in size and vast in significance.

I belong to the infinitely unfolding whole.

Meditation 4 — The Path of Compassion

May you know peace.

May you find clarity.

May your suffering ease.

May the Spirit Field guide you toward harmony.

May I love without condition, as compassion is my true nature.

Meditation 5 — The Spirit Within All Things

In this moment, nothing is missing.

The Spirit Field flows through my awareness.

I am connected to the Earth beneath and the cosmos above.

I am whole in this breath, and every breath.

I rest in the unity of existence.

These affirmations and meditations are designed to be spoken slowly, adapted gently, and used without coercion. Their value lies in rhythm, repetition, and reflective steadiness rather than performance.

Conclusion — The Practice of Resonance

Volume IV gathers the most directly usable strands of the SDAE corpus into one place. It is not the formal metaphysical companion of Volume II, nor the scriptural and memorial companion of Volume III. It is the book of repetition: the place where coherence is practiced in body, attention, relationship, and responsibility.

Its themes repeat because practice repeats. Nature, stillness, relationship, coherence, truthfulness, purpose, compassion, and wonder do not become real by being admired once. They become real through rhythm.

The practical claim of Volume IV is modest but serious: a human being can become more coherent. The body can be steadied. The mind can be clarified. Relationship can be repaired. Pressure can be named. Dignity can be defended. The work is not linear, but it is real.

Appendix A — Gentle Use, Safety, and Scope

This practice book is not therapy, diagnosis, medicine, or emergency support. It can accompany such care, but it should not replace it. Exercises involving grief, trauma, discrimination, difficult relationships, or intense stress should be approached gently. If a practice intensifies distress rather than clarifying it, stop and seek appropriate support.

The language of Spirit Field, resonance, coherence, orbit, and curvature in this volume is practical and phenomenological. It is not a claim about hidden physics, energy transfer, or medical certainty. Use the materials slowly. Adapt them to actual life. Let the practices serve dignity rather than performance.

Appendix B — Notes on Care Guides and More Intensive Regimens

This expanded Volume IV intentionally keeps its focus on daily practice, regulation, reflection, and resilience. More intervention-specific materials—especially fasting doctrines, "bounce" schedules, clinical nutrition protocols, or product-centered rebuilding strategies—should remain in separate NuSpecies care guides or clinician-reviewed support materials rather than in the core practice book.

That boundary protects the spirit of Volume IV: gentle use, honest limits, science-respecting language, and practices that ordinary readers can repeat without overreach.